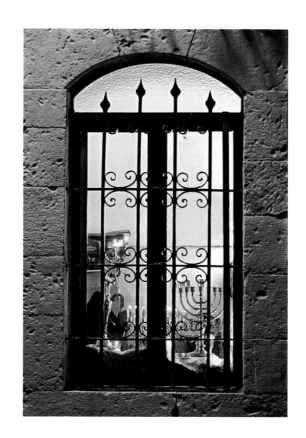

Celebrate Hanukkah

Deborah Heiligman
Consultant, Rabbi Shira Stern

NATIONAL GEOGRAPHIC
WASHINGTON, D.C.

This Israeli boy is lighting his Hanukkiah
on the 8th night of Hanukkah.

light

latkes

In late November or in December, Jewish people all over the world celebrate Hanukkah. We celebrate with light, latkes, and dreidels.

We hear the story of Hanukkah: Two thousand years ago, a wicked king named Antiochus didn't allow Jews to practice their religion. He took over the Temple in Jerusalem where they worshiped. But the Jews fought back.

dreidels

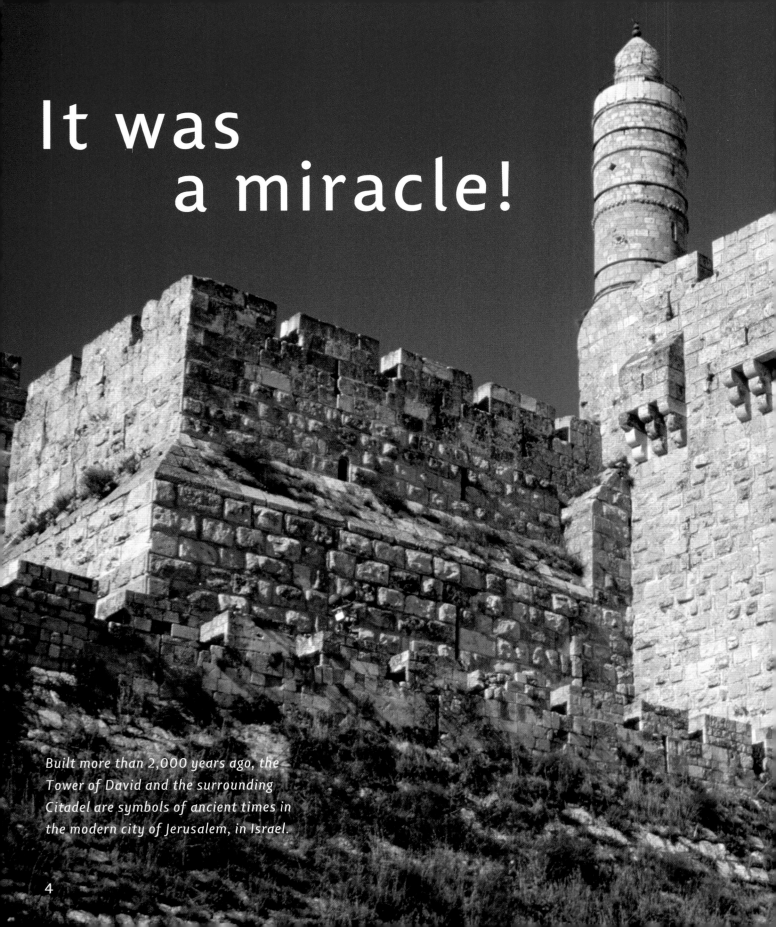

It was
a miracle!

Built more than 2,000 years ago, the
Tower of David and the surrounding
Citadel are symbols of ancient times in
the modern city of Jerusalem, in Israel.

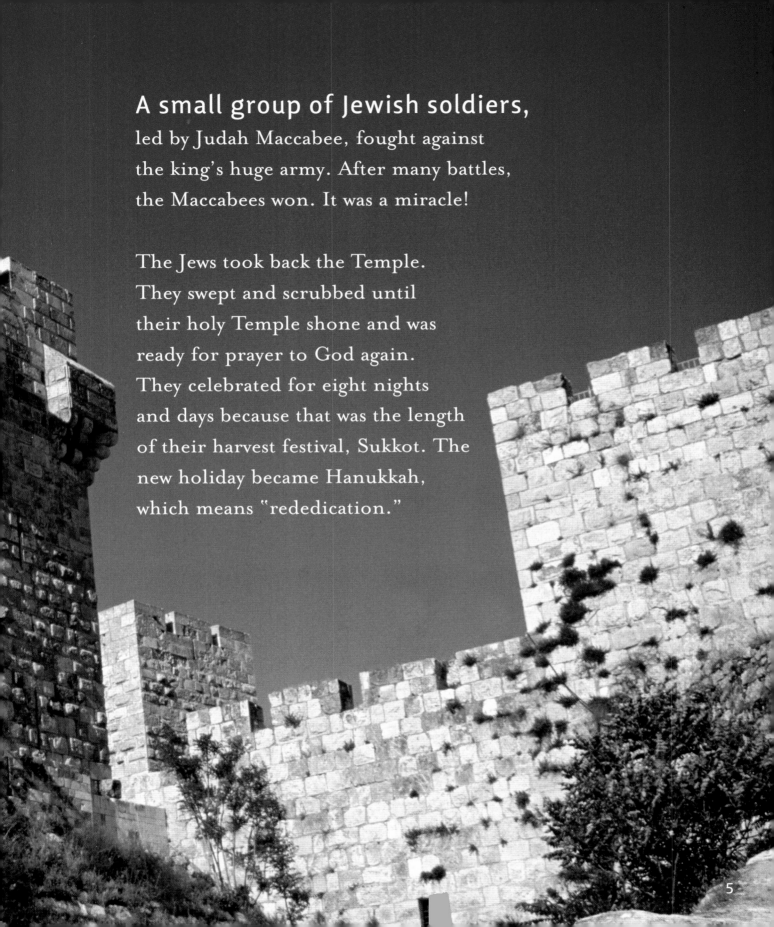

A small group of Jewish soldiers, led by Judah Maccabee, fought against the king's huge army. After many battles, the Maccabees won. It was a miracle!

The Jews took back the Temple. They swept and scrubbed until their holy Temple shone and was ready for prayer to God again. They celebrated for eight nights and days because that was the length of their harvest festival, Sukkot. The new holiday became Hanukkah, which means "rededication."

We still celebrate

Hanukkah for eight nights and days. Hanukkah begins at sundown like all Jewish holidays. Each night we light candles in a special candleholder called a Hanukkah menorah, or *Hanukkiah.*

The Hanukkiah has nine candles. There is a candle for every night, plus a helper candle, called a *shamash.* We use the shamash to light the other candles.

Each night we light candles.

Michael Ohayon lights a 13-foot-high, 10-foot-wide Hanukkah menorah during an outdoor Hanukkah celebration in Jacksonville, Florida.

In Jerusalem, an Orthodox Jewish boy lights a Hanukkiah made of oil lamps inside a glass box that is displayed outside the house.

On the first night

we light one candle with the shamash. On the second night we light two candles with the shamash, on the third three, and so on. The candles bring light to dark, cold nights during Hanukkah, the Festival of Lights.

The Festival of Lights

*Hanukkiah from Ancient Israel,
3rd to 5th Century*

Women in Imphal, India, light Hanukkah candles on a rooftop.

We say prayers every night

when we light candles. On the first night we say a prayer thanking God for letting us reach this happy occasion. On all eight nights we say two other blessings. In one of them, we bless God for commanding us to kindle the Hanukkah lights. In the other, we bless God for making miracles happen.

During Hanukkah a special prayer about miracles is included in the morning prayers. Here, David Salazar of Trujillo, Peru, dons a tallis, or prayer shawl, to pray.

Say a prayer.

Samson Wamani, a member of Uganda's small but strong Jewish community, looks out the window of his home.

We are proud to be Jewish.

It is important to tell about the miracle. We want to show everyone we are proud to be Jewish. We are glad that we are free to practice our religion. That's why all over the world, people put Hanukkiahs in windows and light menorahs in cities and towns and parks.

Hanukkah Card from South Korea, 1951

13

This 26-foot-tall Hanukkiah stands in front of the Palace of Culture in Warsaw, Poland.

We are happy to celebrate

another miracle of Hanukkah, too,
the miracle of the oil. Over the years,
people told a story about the first
Hanukkah. They said that when the Jews
went to light a special oil lamp, there was
only a tiny bit of sacred oil, enough for
just one night. But they were supposed to
light that lamp and celebrate the holiday
for eight nights. It would take too long for
them to get more oil. What could they do?

*Oil Lamp from Egypt,
7th Century*

Then another miracle happened.

Then another miracle happened:
The tiny bit of oil lasted for eight nights.
We celebrate that miracle today.
We celebrate by eating…

Delicious!

A girl makes latkes with her mother and sister for their family in Los Angeles, California.

We eat foods made with oil.

We make potato pancakes called *latkes*. We grate the potatoes, mix in flour, eggs, and salt, and deep-fry them in oil. Delicious! We eat them with applesauce or sour cream. Or both.

We also eat jelly-filled doughnuts called *sufganiyot*. They are fried in oil. They are delicious, too!

An Israeli soldier enjoys a sufganiya (jelly doughnut) during a break from duty on Mount Hermon in the Golan Heights.

spin,

After dinner we play

with a spinning top called a dreidel.
The Hebrew letters on the sides of
the dreidel stand for "A Great Miracle
Happened There." In Israel the
letters stand for "A Great Miracle
Happened *Here.*"

We play a betting game with the
dreidel. If you win, you get to take
the pot of raisins or nuts or pennies.
If you lose, you have to put yours
back. Sometimes you get half, and
sometimes you get nothing.

spin,

Dreidels are also fun just to spin,
spin, spin...

spin...

Children play with dreidels in front of
their family's store in Ghana, West Africa.

We put on Hanukkah plays, and we sing songs. We give and get presents, too. Some children get a present on each night of Hanukkah. Some get one big present on the last night. We get *gelt,* or money, as well. But we also think of others who have less than we do. We give *tzedakah,* or charity, to those who are needy.

We sing songs.

Greta Peterson, Mushka Cohen, and Elisheva Elzhasadeh sing during a menorah-lighting ceremony in Sacramento, California.

We share the light
in our hearts.

Like all Jewish holidays, Hanukkah is a time to be with family and friends. It's also a time to open up our homes to those who are alone. We invite them to celebrate with us. We share the light in our hearts.

Igaal, Dafuna, and Simcha celebrate together in Uganda.

All over the world we celebrate

the miracles of Hanukkah. We can practice our religion. We are free!

On the last night of Hanukkah all of the candles are blazing. Our world is filled with light.

Acrobat Laura Luciani twirls a wheel of fire at a Hanukkah celebration in Rome, Italy.

Our
world
is
filled
with
light.

MORE ABOUT HANUKKAH

Contents

Just the Facts

WHO CELEBRATES IT: Jews

WHAT IT IS: A holiday to celebrate two miracles: the victory of Judah Maccabee's army over the army of King Antiochus and a little bit of sacred oil lasting eight days.

WHEN IT STARTS: The 25th day of the Hebrew month Kislev, which sometimes occurs in late November but which is usually in December.

HOW LONG: Hanukkah lasts eight days and nights. Like all Jewish holidays, it begins at sundown.

ALSO KNOWN AS: The Festival of Lights. The word "Hanukkah" means "rededication."

RITUAL: Lighting the candles on the Hanukkah menorah (Hanukkiah) is the most important ritual.

FOOD: Foods made with oil, especially latkes (potato pancakes) and sufganiyot (jelly doughnuts). Some people also eat foods made with cheese.

How to Light a Menorah

HANUKKAH CANDLES are put in the menorah from right to left, with the newest candle added to the left. Then they are lit from left to right. The eight candles should all be the same height, with the ninth candle, the shamash, higher. The candles should be tall enough to burn for at least half an hour.

It is a nice custom for each person in the family to have a Hanukkah menorah to light.

Before we light the Hanukkah menorah, we say these blessings:

Blessed are You, Lord our God,
the sovereign of all worlds, who has made us holy
with your commandments, and
commanded us to kindle the Hanukkah lights.

Blessed are You, Lord our God,
the sovereign of all worlds,
who accomplished miracles for our ancestors
in ancient days, and in our time.

The *Shehecheyanu*
(Recited only on the first night)
Blessed are You, Lord our God,
the sovereign of all worlds,
who has given us life, kept us strong,
and brought us to this joyous occasion.

Deborah's Potato Latkes

ONE RECIPE makes about 20 good-size latkes. I triple the batch for a main course for 10 latke-loving people.

INGREDIENTS:
6 medium potatoes, peeled
1 onion
1 teaspoon salt
1 egg, beaten
3 tablespoons flour
$1/2$ teaspoon baking powder

YOU WILL ALSO NEED:
paper towels
brown paper bags, ripped into sheets to
   put in oven

1. Grate potatoes on large holes of hand grater. (Some people use a food processor, but the texture just doesn't come out right!)

2. Drain potato juice: Put the grated potatoes in a colander in the sink or over a bowl. Use your hands to squish and squeeze all the juice out. (This is a very important part of the recipe and a great job for kids!)

3. Grate the onion on large holes, drain it, and add it to the potato. (You're going to cry onion tears when you grate the onion. You might want to wear goggles!)

4. Put the drained potato and onion mixture into a big bowl. Add egg and salt, mix with a big spoon; add baking powder and flour, mix well with the same spoon.

5. Heat oil in frying pan or electric skillet—there should be enough oil to almost cover the latkes. (This is a job for adults.) When the oil is hot, spoon in the "batter" to make the size latkes you like. Brown on each side until nice and crispy.

6. Take the latkes out of the pan and place them on paper towels to drain some of the grease. After a few minutes, transfer them to brown paper in a warm oven (250°F) until all the latkes are done.

7. Eat the latkes! Serve them with applesauce or sour cream, or both.

Playing Dreidel

LONG, LONG AGO when the Jews were not allowed to practice their religion, they did anyway—in secret. When they studied Torah (the Jewish holy book), they took spinning tops with them. If soldiers came upon them, the Jews would take out the tops and pretend they were just playing betting games, not studying Torah.

The Hebrew letters on the dreidel stand for "A Great Miracle Happened There." In Israel they stand for "A Great Miracle Happened Here."

U.S. astronaut Jeffrey Hoffman brought a dreidel and a menorah onto the space shuttle Endeavor *during a mission in December, 1993. He couldn't light candles because the spark could ignite the oxygen in the orbiter, causing it to explode. But he did spin the dreidel in zero gravity. "It was quite fun," he says. "It spins forever!"*

How to Play Dreidel

Get two or more players. Give each person the same number of game pieces. You can use pennies, raisins, chocolate candy, nuts, toothpicks, or whatever you want.

Everyone puts one game piece into the center, or the pot. (Do the same every time the pot is emptied, or when there is only one piece left.)

Take turns spinning the dreidel. When it's your turn, spin it once. When it stops, see what letter it lands on. Then follow these directions:

- If it lands on **Nun**, do nothing.

- If it lands on **Gimmel**, you get everything in the pot.

- If it lands on **Hay**, you get half the pot. (If it's an odd number, you get the extra one in the pot.)

- If it lands on **Shin** (or **Peh** if you're in Israel), add a piece to the pot.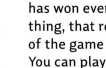

- When you run out of pieces, you are out of the game.

- When one person has won everything, that round of the game is over. You can play again!

- If you play with real money, it would be in the spirit of Hanukkah to donate your winnings to charity.

Find Out More

There are many, many books and Web sites about Hanukkah. Below are some you might enjoy reading to learn more about the holiday. The books with stars (*) are especially good for children.

Note that there are also many ways to *spell* the name of this holiday in the English language. When you do research, remember to try alternate spellings, including Chanukah, Chanukkah, and Hanukah.

BOOKS

Helderman, Jennie Miller and Mary Caulkins, *Hanukkah Trivia: 150 Fun & Fascinating Facts About Hanukkah.* Gramercy Books, 2002. A fun book to look at. For older children and adults.

Kolatch, Alfred J., *The Jewish Book of Why.* Jonathan David Publishers, 2000. This is a good resource for adults.

* Rosen, Michael J., *Our Eight Nights of Hanukkah.* Illustrated by Dyanne Disalvo Ryan. Holiday House, 2000. A lovely book about how one family celebrates Hanukkah.

* Simon, Norma, *The Story of Hanukkah.* Illustrated by Leonid Gore. HarperCollins, 1997. A very good nonfiction book about Hanukkah.

Telushkin, Rabbi Joseph, *Jewish Literacy: The Most Important Things to Know About the Jewish Religion, Its People, and Its History.* William Morrow and Company, 1991. This is a terrific book for adults about all of Judaism. Easy to use and understand.

* Zalben, Jane Breskin, *Pearl's Eight Days of Chanukah.* Simon and Schuster Books for Young Readers, 1998. This is a wonderful book with a story and activity for each night of Hanukkah. It is fiction, but has good information and crafts to do to celebrate the holiday.

WEB SITES

There are many, many Web sites about Hanukkah. As with all Internet research, be careful. Accuracy can be a problem. Here are a few sites that you might find helpful.

www.hanukkah.org
To listen to the Hanukkah blessings, click here. This site, put out by the Chabad Lubavitch movement, has a wealth of interesting information.

www.history.com/topics/holidays/ hanukkah
The History Channel Online has a nice set of pages about the history of Hanukkah, traditions, and some trivia. This is a great site for older children and adults.

www.holidays.net/chanukah/
This is a good Web site with activities, songs, and information.

www.ucalgary.ca/~elsegal/ Shokel/041209_8Days.html
This is an interesting academic article about why Hanukkah lasts eight days. For those adults who want to delve deeper.

http://urj.org/educate/parent
This is a good resource for parents from the Union for Reform Judaism. There is information on all Jewish holidays, including Hanukkah.

EDUCATIONAL EXTENSIONS

Reading

1. Why do Jews celebrate Hanukkah by eating foods made with oil?

2. Hanukkah means "rededication," and the holiday is also referred to as "The Festival of Lights." How do these terms reflect the spirit of the holiday?

3. Pick a favorite photograph from the text and reread its caption. What symbols of Hanukkah can you see in the details of the image? (Hint: Expand upon the information given and the details observed visually in relation to the context of the page.)

Writing

4. Write an informative/explanatory essay about the use of the dreidel during Hanukkah. Explain the role of the dreidel in ancient times and what it symbolizes for the Jews.

Speaking & Listening

5. Present your explanatory essay to your class, friends, or parents. Make your own dreidel (and possibly gelt or something else you might bet with) to use as a visual display of the information you are presenting.

Glossary

Dreidel: four-sided spinning top children play with on Hanukkah. "Dreidel" is the Yiddish word for "turn."

Gelt: money. A traditional Hanukkah gift, which can be real or chocolate money.

Hanukkiah: candleholder with nine candles used specially on Hanukkah. The plural is Hanukkiot, or Hanukkiahs.

Hebrew: language of the Jewish bible. It is also the language spoken by Jews in Israel today.

Latkes: potato pancakes

Menorah: candleholder with any number of candles. It is often a synonym for Hanukkiah.

Shamash: servant candle used to light the other candles on the Hanukkiah. "Shamash" means "servant" in Hebrew.

Sufganiya: jelly doughnut. The plural is sufganiyot.

Tzedakah: charity

Yiddish: language spoken by Jewish people of eastern and central European descent. It is a combination of German, Hebrew, and other languages. At one time it was spoken by more Jews than any other language.

Where This Book's Photos Were Taken

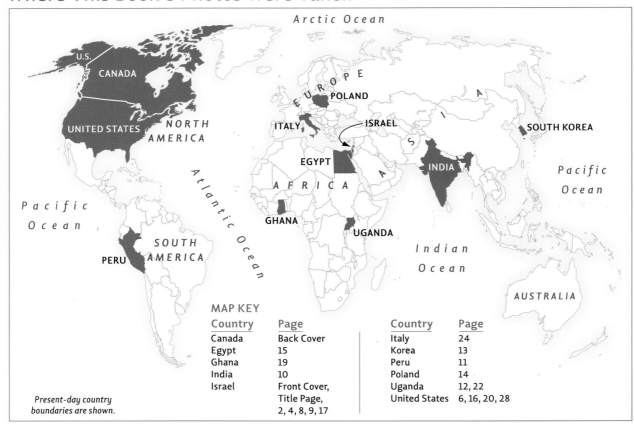

Present-day country boundaries are shown.

MAP KEY

Country	Page
Canada	Back Cover
Egypt	15
Ghana	19
India	10
Israel	Front Cover, Title Page, 2, 4, 8, 9, 17

Country	Page
Italy	24
Korea	13
Peru	11
Poland	14
Uganda	12, 22
United States	6, 16, 20, 28

Hanukkah: Its Meaning and Message

by Rabbi Shira Stern

It's no coincidence that the story and the celebration of Hanukkah coincide with the Christian holiday of Christmas: They both are meant to "lighten" up the darkest days of winter, when it's scary and cold, and the days get shorter and the nights longer. But though Christmas is a big deal for Christians, whether you mark it religiously or with a tree and presents, Hanukkah is a minor holiday for Jews. Because Christmas is such a major holiday all over the world, some people make Hanukkah just as significant. However it is actually much less important than the holidays of Rosh Hashanah and Yom Kippur, Passover, Sukkot, Shavuot, and the weekly Sabbath. Sometimes people try to make Hanukkah similar to Christmas, putting up Hanukkah bushes and Hanukkah stockings, but this takes away what is unique about each holiday, for each one belongs to a different tradition.

The story and tradition of Hanukkah comes from Jewish history. In the second century B.C.E. (before the common era), the Syrian Greeks had control over the land of Israel, with King Antiochus IV ruling over the Jews. During this time, Jews weren't allowed to celebrate their Sabbath or their holidays, study religious texts, or circumcise their children, on pain of death. They were even banned from entering their Holy Temple.

While some Jews accepted these strict laws, others—the Hasmoneans with Judah Maccabee (the Hammer) as their leader—fought to preserve their traditions and stay Jewish. After three years of hard battles, the Maccabees succeeded in taking back Jerusalem, against a huge Syrian army. They cleaned out the Temple that the Greeks had defiled by putting up statues and sacrificing (actually barbequing) pork on the altar. They relit the light that was never supposed to go out, and sat down to celebrate the most important holiday to a farming community: the week-long harvest festival of Sukkot.

The next year, in 164 B.C.E., they had Sukkot at the right time in September/October, but they wanted to do something special to remember their victory. So they created another eight-day holiday, dedicated to... "rededication," which is what the word "Hanukkah" actually means.

You may know the other story about Hanukkah: about the small amount of oil that miraculously lasted an entire week. Each story was meant to tell us something different: The military story really shows how a few people with a dream can achieve their goal when they work together[1], and the oil story reminds us that God can make miracles happen[2], bringing light into the world and giving us strength. Sometimes we forget that the power of a single, tiny flame can illumine the darkness and dispel much more than the gloom.

We keep alive the stories of Hanukkah because we are now the keepers of the flame. So we light candles each night of the holiday and sing about the miracles, both human and divine. One small light made their eight-day celebration a joyous one, and ours as well; from then until now, that small light continues to grow every time family and friends participate in making Hanukkah happen.

Rabbi Shira Stern is a pastoral counselor and chaplain in Marlboro, N.J., and director of the Center for Pastoral Care and Counseling.

---

1 Read about the military victory in the first two books of the Maccabees, which can be found in the Apocrypha, the "extra books" preserved by the early Christian Church that are sandwiched between the Hebrew Bible and the New Testament. Go to *http://www.earlyjewishwritings.com.* Scroll down to Deuterocanon and click on 1 and 2 Maccabees.

2 Find out about the miracle of oil in a story preserved in the Talmud, the Jewish Law books (Shabbat 21b). See *http://www.sacred-texts.com/jud/t01/t0110.htm.*

For Mea, who saved the latkes that year

PICTURE CREDITS

Front Cover © Lori Epstein/National Geographic Creative; Back Cover © Arina Habich/Alamy; Spine © Lori Epstein/National Geographic Creative; page 1 © Olivier Fitoussi/BauBau; page 2 © Yehoshua Halevi/Golden Light Images; page 3 (top) © Leigh Beisch/Getty Images; (bottom) © Scott Rothstein/ Shutterstock; pages 4–5 © James Marshall/ Corbis; pages 6–7 © Will Dickey/ The Florida Times Union/AP Wide World; page 8 © Hanan Ischar/Holy Land Images; page 9 The Jewish Museum, NY/Art Resource; pages 10 & 11 © Bryan Schwartz; pages 12–13 © Richard Sobol/ZUMA Press; page 13 (right) The Jewish Museum, NY/Art Resource; page 14 © Czarek Sokolowski/AP Wide World Photos; page 15 Snark/ Art Resource; page 16 © Bill Aron/Ponka Wonka. com; page 17 © Yael Bar Hillel/IDF/Getty Images; page 18 (top) © Ingram Publishing/Foto Search; (center) © PhotoDisc/ Getty Images; (bottom) © Erich Lessing/Art Resource; page 19 © Bryan Schwartz; page 20 © Lezlie Sterling/Sacramento Bee/ZUMA Press; page 21 (top) © Lisa C. McDonald/ Shutterstock; (bottom) © Scott Rothstein/Shutterstock; pages 22–23 © E. Weinstein/ PonkaWonka.com; pages 24–25 © Giulio Napolitano/AFP/ Getty Images; page 27 © Ben Fink/FoodPix/ PictureArts; page 28 (top) Courtesy NASA; (bottom) © Scott Rothstein/ Shutterstock

Text copyright © 2006 Deborah Heiligman
Compilation copyright © 2006 National Geographic Society
Reprinted in paperback and library binding, 2016
Published by National Geographic Partners, LLC
All rights reserved. Reproduction of the whole or any part of the contents without written permission from the publisher is prohibited.

The Library of Congress cataloged the 2006 edition as follows:

Heiligman, Deborah.
Celebrate Hanukkah / Deborah Heiligman ; consultant, Shira Stern.
    p. cm.— (Holidays Around the World)
ISBN 0-7922-5924-6 (hardcover)
ISBN 0-7922-5925-4 (library binding)
1. Hanukkah — Juvenile literature. I. Title. II. Series: Holidays around the world (National Geographic Society (U.S.)

BM695.H3H446 2006
296.4'35 — dc22

                                        2005032427

2016 paperback edition ISBN: 978-1-4263-2476-5
2016 reinforced library binding edition ISBN: 978-1-4263-2477-2

National Geographic supports K–12 educators with ELA Common Core Resources. Visit natgeoed.org/commoncore for more information.

Front cover: A girl uses the *shamash* to light a menorah.
Back cover: Hanukkah gelt and dreidels

Since 1888, the National Geographic Society has funded more than 12,000 research, exploration, and preservation projects around the world. The Society receives funds from National Geographic Partners, LLC, funded in part by your purchase. A portion of the proceeds from this book supports this vital work.

NATIONAL GEOGRAPHIC and Yellow Border Design are trademarks of the National Geographic Society, used under license.

For more information, please visit nationalgeographic.com, call 1-800-647-5463, or write to the following address:
National Geographic Partners, LLC
1145 17th Street N.W., Washington, D.C. 20036-4688 U.S.A.

For information about special discounts for bulk purchases, please contact National Geographic Books Special Sales: ngspecsales@ngs.org

For rights or permissions inquiries, please contact National Geographic Books Subsidiary Rights: ngbookrights@ngs.org

STAFF FOR THIS BOOK
Nancy Laties Feresten, *Vice President, Editor-in-Chief of Children's Books*
Jennifer Emmett, Sue Macy, *Project Editors*
Jim Hiscott, *Art Director*
Callie Broaddus, *Associate Designer*
Lori Epstein, *Illustrations Editor*
Carl Mehler, *Director of Maps*
Priyanka Lamichhane, *Editorial Assistant*
Rebecca Hinds, *Managing Editor*
Paige Towler, *Editorial Assistant*
R. Gary Colbert, *Production Director*
Lewis R. Bassford, *Production Manager*
Vincent P. Ryan, Maryclare Tracy, *Manufacturing Managers*
Kelsey Carlson, *Education Consultant*

Printed in Hong Kong
16/THK/1

Book design is by 3+Co.
The body text in the book is set in Mrs. Eaves.
The display text is in Lisboa.

ACKNOWLEDGMENTS
With thanks to Rabbi Don Weber for his insights and advice; to Eytan Stern Weber, future astronaut, for explaining to me why it wouldn't be safe to light candles in space; to Professor Jerome Weiner for a spirited debate; and to the Sandbergs, Schiff-Glenns, and Forman-Greenwalds who eat my latkes and help us celebrate Hanukkah.